To the Reader...

Our purpose in creating this series is to provide young readers with accurate accounts of the lives of Native American men and women important in the history of their tribes. The stories are written by scholars, including American Indians.

Native Americans are as much a part of North American life today as they were one hundred years ago. Even in times past, Indians were not all the same. Not all of them lived in teepees or wore feather warbonnets. They were not all warriors. Some did fight against the white man, but many befriended him.

Whether patriot or politician, athlete or artist, Arapaho or Zuni, the story of each person in this series deserves to be told. Whether the individuals gained distinction on the battlefield or the playing field, in the courtroom or the classroom, they have enriched the heritage and history of all Americans. It is hoped that those who read their stories will realize that many different peoples, regardless of culture or color, have played a part in shaping the United States and Canada, in making both countries what they are today.

> Herman J. Viola
> General Editor
> Author of *Exploring the West*
> and other volumes on the West
> and Native Americans

GENERAL EDITOR

Herman J. Viola
Author of *Exploring the West* and other volumes on the West
and Native Americans

MANAGING EDITOR

Robert M. Kvasnicka
Coeditor of *The Commissioners of Indian Affairs, 1824-1977*
Coeditor of *Indian-White Relations: A Persistent Paradox*

MANUSCRIPT EDITOR

Eric Newman

PROJECT MANAGER

Joyce Spicer

PRODUCTION

Jack Reichard
Scott Melcer

Published by Steck-Vaughn 1993

Copyright © 1993 Pinnacle Press, Inc., doing business as Rivilo Books

Printed and bound in the United States.

1 2 3 4 5 6 7 8 9 0   WO   98 97 96 95 94 93

Library of Congress Cataloging-in-Publication Data

Viola, Herman J.
      Osceola / text written by Herman J. Viola; illustrations by
Yoshi Miyake
          p.   cm. — (American Indian stories)
      "A Rivilo Book."
      Summary: A biography of the American Indian leader who
fought the United States government's attempts to remove the
Seminoles from their homeland.
          ISBN 0-8114-6575-6   —   ISBN 0-8114-4098-2 (soft cover)
      1. Osceola, Seminole chief, 1804-1838 — Juvenile literature.
2. Seminole Indians — Biography — Juvenile literature.
3. Seminole Indians — History — Juvenile literature.   4. Seminole
Indians — Wars — Juvenile literature.   [1. Osceola, Seminole
chief, 1804-1838.   2. Seminole Indians — Biography.   3. Indians
of North America — Biography.]   I. Miyake, Yoshi, ill.   II. Title.
III. Series.
E99.S28086   1993
973.5'4'092 — dc20
      [B]   92-5683
                                                            CIP AC

OSCEOLA

Text by Herman J. Viola
Illustrations by Yoshi Miyake

A RIVILO BOOK

RSVP
RAINTREE
STECK-VAUGHN
PUBLISHERS
The Steck-Vaughn Company

The early life of Osceola (Ŏs-cē-ō-la), the great Seminole leader, is rather mysterious. Like other famous Indians who lived long ago, little is known about his childhood. He was born about 1804 in a village near the Tallapoosa River in what is today Alabama. His parents were Creek Indians, but one of his grandfathers was a white man. After Osceola's father died, his mother married a white man named William Powell. As a young boy, Osceola was known as Billy Powell. He received his Indian name after his mother left her husband and moved with her son to Florida, probably late in 1814. There they joined the Seminole Indian tribe.

Osceola's Indian name was really *Asi-Yaholo*. *Asi* means "black drink," a special beverage that the Seminoles made for certain ceremonies. *Yaholo* means "singer." The "black drink singer" was the man who called out the names of men when it was their turn to take a drink. Because Asi-Yaholo was hard for white people to say, they mispronounced it as Osceola.

Not only is Osceola's early life mysterious, but the early history of the Seminole Indians is also. The Seminoles are actually a mixture of many peoples—Indians, blacks, and whites who lived with the Indians. The name Seminole means "runaway" in the Creek language. Most of the early Seminoles were Creek Indians who had "run away" from their homeland in Georgia and Alabama to live in Florida. The Indians left their homeland because white people had moved into it, taking the Indians' land for themselves. When the Indians tried to fight to keep their homes, they usually were defeated because the whites had more soldiers and better weapons. In fact, Osceola and his mother went to Florida with Indians who had sided with Britain against the United States in the War of 1812. The Indians fled to Florida after being defeated by General Andrew Jackson at Horseshoe Bend, Alabama, in an important battle fought during the last year of the war.

When the Indians went into Florida they entered a foreign land. Until 1819 Florida was owned by Spain. When the first groups of Creek Indians began moving into Florida about 1750, most of the whites who lived there were located in settlements on the coast. Only a few scattered groups of Indians lived in the interior part of Florida.

The runaway Creek Indians thought Florida was a good place to live. The land with its many rivers, swamps, marshy areas covered with tall grass, and jungle areas made it easy to hide from the whites. The mosquitoes, snakes, and alligators that lived there also made the land less desirable to the whites.

The Creek Indians liked the hot weather. It was easy to grow crops such as corn and potatoes because the soil was very fertile and the growing season was very long. There were many animals, such as deer and rabbits, to hunt, and it was easy to catch fish. The Indians built grass houses on stilts to keep them up off the damp ground. Called "chickees," the grass houses were easy to make. Usually they had no walls—only a floor and a roof held up by corner poles.

Runaway slaves also went to Florida for the same reasons the Indians did. Before slavery was ended in the 1860s, some white people kept black people as slaves. Many blacks tried to run away from the people who owned them. Some ran north, trying to reach Canada, a country that did not allow slavery. Other slaves who lived close to Florida went there. Some lived with the Indians, who welcomed them and protected them. Others set up their own towns.

By the time Osceola and his mother arrived in Florida, many runaway Creek Indians, some blacks, and some of the Indian groups that had always lived in Florida had already joined together. They were known as the Seminole tribe. The Seminoles continued to welcome the other Indians and slaves who fled from the United States. The fact that the Indians helped the slaves made the white slaveholders in the United States very angry.

Osceola and his mother had been in Florida about three years when the first war between the United States and the Seminole Indians began. In 1817 United States soldiers crossed into Florida to arrest a Seminole chief who had been hiding slaves. The soldiers killed five Indians and burned the chief's town. Later, when some Indians took revenge by attacking some soldiers, the United States government decided that the Seminoles should be punished.

In March 1818 General Andrew Jackson led a large military force into Florida. He attacked the village where Osceola lived. The soldiers killed 37 Indians and captured over 100 others, including Osceola and his mother. Because the soldiers could not care for so many prisoners, Jackson let the captives go. Once again, Osceola and his mother had to look for another place to live.

Jackson's troops marched through northern Florida, burning Indian villages and capturing two Spanish cities. He also hanged two British citizens and almost provoked a war with Great Britain and Spain. In February 1819, Spain turned Florida over to the United States. The First Seminole War was over. Those Indians who had fled into Florida to get away from the United States were once again in United States territory.

Many white slaveowners now wanted the United States government to make the Seminoles return all the black people living with them. They wanted to make the black people slaves again. The whites also wanted the government to move the Seminoles, from Florida to an area west of the Mississippi River known as Indian Territory, now part of Oklahoma. They thought that once the Seminoles were gone the slaves no longer could run away and find shelter with them. Instead, the government made a treaty with the Indians in 1823. The Seminoles, agreed to live on a reservation, a large tract of land in central Florida. A government agent would look after them there, and a police force would make sure that no more runaway slaves joined the Indians.

By this time Osceola was a young man. He was respected as a hunter and a warrior, and he served as the "tustenuggee," or military leader, of his small band. In 1825 he and his band moved to the reservation. There, Osceola helped Micanopy, the main chief of the Seminoles, to keep order on the reservation. He even helped the Indian agent capture Indians who left the reservation.

The Indians were not happy on the reservation. The government had selected some of the poorest land in Florida for their home. They could not raise enough food for their needs. There were few animals to hunt. Because they were not allowed to leave the reservation to hunt in other areas, the Indians often went hungry.

The Indians became even more unhappy when white slave catchers came onto the reservation to reclaim slaves. The Seminoles, did not want to return the blacks. Many of the blacks the slave catchers wanted were married to Indians, and others had been born free and had never been slaves.

The whites became more determined than ever that the Seminoles had to leave Florida. After Andrew Jackson became President of the United States in 1829, Congress passed the Indian Removal Bill. It called for all the Indians who lived in the South to be moved to Indian Territory. In 1832 men from the government held a meeting with the Seminole leaders to get them to agree to move. Osceola attended the meeting; he was there to keep order and to protect the white officials if trouble started. He was not yet important enough to sign the treaty that was made.

Under the terms of the treaty the Seminoles sent some of their leaders to Indian Territory to find a suitable place for the tribe to live. While the leaders were in the West the agent had them sign another agreement saying that they had found a place they liked. The leaders did not realize that the new agreement required all the Seminoles to leave Florida whenever the government was ready to move them to Indian Territory.

When the Seminoles found out what the agreement really meant they were very angry. They did not want to leave Florida for a land they did not know. They did not trust the whites and were afraid of what would happen to them if they moved. Some of the Seminoles decided to stay in Florida and to fight the United States Army if necessary. Their leader was Osceola.

Like most Seminoles, Osceola felt no real loyalty to the United States. Florida was his home. Florida, not the United States, was his country. He did not intend to be forced to move again. He now began telling the chiefs of the various bands that they should refuse to move.

Osceola had made some white friends. One of his closest friends was an army officer. When the fighting began again he told his warriors not to harm the officer. Osceola also was friendly with the new Indian agent, a man named Wiley Thompson. Thompson lived in Fort King, an army post that was located very close to the Seminole villages.

Thompson had been appointed in 1833 by the United States government to look after the Indians. As their agent, it was his job to protect them. It was also his job to see that they moved out of Florida, but the Indians did not immediately realize that.

Thompson held a meeting with the Seminole leaders, including Osceola, in October 1834. He told them that the time had come for them to make plans for their move to Indian Territory. They would have to leave Florida by the following spring. He allowed the Indians to hold their own meeting to discuss this news, but he planted a spy among them. The spy told him that Osceola had urged the leaders to resist the move. Later, however, when Thompson met with the Indians again, Osceola came forward and announced that the Indians would not move. They intended to stay in Florida.

In April 1835 Thompson again ordered the Seminole leaders to come to the fort. This time he had some army officers with him remind the Indians that they could be forced to do what the government wanted. He told them to sign a paper saying that they would begin leaving Florida in January 1836.

The leaders did not want to sign the paper, but many of them were afraid to refuse. One by one, each man made his mark on the paper with a goose-quill pen. Finally, it was Osceola's turn. Everyone watched to see what he would do. They knew that he was angry because he had said nothing during the meeting. Slowly Osceola walked to the table that held the paper. He stared at Thompson. Instead of reaching for the pen, Osceola pulled out his hunting knife and stuck it in the table.

"This is the only way I sign!" he yelled. Then he put his knife back in its sheath and walked away.

Thompson wanted to punish Osceola for not signing the agreement. Because many of the Seminoles now looked to Osceola for leadership, Thompson was worried that Osceola would cause trouble when the government began moving the Indians out of Florida. One day when Osceola came to the fort to buy supplies, he and Thompson began arguing loudly. Thompson ordered the soldiers at the fort to arrest Osceola. It took four men to hold Osceola so he could be handcuffed. Thompson then had him locked in a jail cell.

Osceola knew that he could get out of jail if he agreed to sign the paper. Thompson told him that he had to sign it in front of all the people from his village. Thompson gave Osceola five days to bring his followers to the fort so that they could see him sign the paper. When Osceola agreed, Thompson freed him.

Osceola kept his word. Five days later he returned with his people. In front of everyone, he signed the hated paper.

Osceola was now very angry. He vowed to get even with Thompson for putting him in jail. Any friendly feelings he had for the agent were forgotten. He began urging his people to fight rather than leave Florida. Many of the young Seminole warriors agreed with Osceola, and he began training them in ways to fight the white soldiers.

The black people who lived with the Seminoles agreed with Osceola as well. They knew that if they were captured the whites would try to make them slaves again. One of the important black leaders was Abraham, an ex-slave who was Chief Micanopy's advisor and interpreter. In order to strengthen the Indian forces, Abraham began secretly visiting the slaves who worked on plantations owned by the whites. He tried to convince the slaves to join the Indians. After the fighting began, the blacks became some of Osceola's strongest allies and best fighters.

The Second Seminole War began in December 1835. Under Osceola's direction the Indians launched three attacks against the whites within one week. On Christmas Day one group of Indians attacked some of the plantations, forcing the whites to abandon the area. Three days later, Osceola got his revenge against Thompson. Osceola led a small group of black and Indian warriors to Fort King. There they hid, waiting for a chance to kill Osceola's enemy. When Thompson and another man left the fort to go for a walk, the Indians killed both men and then escaped before the troops at the fort could catch them.

Meanwhile, some miles away, other Indians and blacks in Osceola's army were fighting a great battle with soldiers who were on their way to Fort King. The soldiers were guided by a black who probably had given the Indians information about the march. When the Indians began firing at the soldiers, the guide slipped away and joined the Seminole warriors. After killing Thompson, Osceola and his men rushed to the site of the battle. They arrived in time to celebrate the Seminoles' greatest victory over the United States Army. The Indian army had killed over one hundred soldiers; only three warriors were killed.

These Seminole victories only made the whites more determined to defeat the Indians. More and more soldiers were sent to Florida. They hunted the Indians with dogs. They captured their villages and burned their food supplies. The soldiers gave the Seminoles no rest. No matter how many soldiers the Indians killed, more came to take their places. The Indians fought so bravely and Osceola led them so capably that many whites outside of Florida came to admire him. They began to feel sorry for the Indians who were fighting so hard to remain in their homeland.

The war dragged on for almost two years. It was very hard on the Indians. Osceola was very sad to see his people so hungry, tired, and afraid. Because they did not get enough to eat, many of the Indians became ill. Some died of their illnesses. Finally, even Osceola got sick. He caught malaria, a disease that people who live in swamps and marshes can catch from a certain kind of mosquito.

Osceola wanted to end the fighting. In October 1837 he sent one of his black chiefs to a nearby fort with a message. He said that he was not ready to surrender, but he wanted a truce, a short stop to the fighting, so he and the whites could talk about ending the war. The next day two hundred soldiers came to his village. They found him standing under a large white flag. "We do not want to surrender," Osceola said, "but we do want to make peace."

The soldiers paid no attention to the white flag of truce. Instead, they surrounded the village and told Osceola that he was their prisoner. Osceola did not try to fight. He was tired and sick. He also did not want to see more of his people get hurt. He and his people surrendered.

25

5095

The soldiers took Osceola to the city of St. Augustine, where he was locked in a large room in Fort Marion. The people from his village joined him at the fort. In this group were his two wives and his children. Although he was happy to be with his family, Osceola was a very sick man. He was thin, weak, and often feverish.

Fearful that the prisoners would escape if they remained in Florida, the army moved the Indians to Charleston, South Carolina. Osceola, 120 warriors, and 82 women and children were taken by boat to Fort Moultrie in Charleston harbor. They arrived on New Year's Day, 1838.

By now Osceola was very sick. He was so famous that many artists wanted to paint his picture before he died. One of the artists who visited him was George Catlin, who had painted the portraits of many Indians from all over the United States. Osceola died on January 30, 1838, just two days after Catlin finished his portrait.

Several soldiers, as well as his wives and children, were with Osceola when he died. Osceola died as he had lived, with dignity. Although he was very weak, he asked for his best clothes and weapons. He dressed himself very carefully. Taking red grease, he painted himself for war, covering one-half of his face and neck with it. Then he put three ostrich feathers in his turban. He put his hunting knife in his belt. When everything was ready, he shook hands with every person in the room, including his wives and his children. Then he lay down, crossed his arms over his chest, and died. He was only thirty-four years old.

Osceola was buried near the entrance to Fort Moultrie. His gravestone identifies him as a "Patriot and Warrior." The day after his death, an article in the Charleston newspaper said: "Osceola will be long remembered. There is something in his character not unworthy of the respect of the world." Indeed, it was so.

Osceola is still remembered as one of the great Indian leaders of all time. Most of the Seminoles and the blacks who lived with them eventually were moved to Indian Territory, but Osceola's determined fight for his homeland captured the imagination of Indians and whites alike. Osceola is so admired that at least twenty-two of the fifty states in the United States have places named for him. Cities, counties, lakes, mountains, a park, and a national forest all bear his name. Osceola has truly become a national hero.

HISTORY OF OSCEOLA

Ca. 1804 Osceola was born.

1812-14 Great Britain and the United States fought the War of 1812.

1814 Pro-British Creek Indians fought Andrew Jackson's troops at Horseshoe Bend, Alabama, and lost. Many of the defeated Indians, accompanied by the young Osceola and his mother, left the United States for Florida.

1817-19 The First Seminole War was fought.

1818 Osceola and his mother were captured by Jackson's army, but later released.

1819 The United States acquired Florida from Spain.

1823 The United States government and the Seminole Indians signed a treaty. The Indians agreed to live on a reservation.

1825 Osceola and his band moved to the reservation, where he helped maintain order.

1830 The Indian Removal Act was passed by Congress, allowing the government to move the Southern tribes to a place west of the Mississippi River.

1833 A few Seminole leaders unwittingly signed an agreement committing the entire Seminole Nation to move west of the Mississippi River.

1835 Osceola was jailed by the Indian agent and forced to sign a paper agreeing to removal. The Second Seminole War began. Osceola and his men killed the Indian agent, and Seminole warriors defeated American troops in a major battle.

1837 Soldiers ignored a flag of truce to capture Osceola.

1838 Osceola died while being held prisoner at Fort Moultrie in Charleston, South Carolina.

5095